Kid's Library of Space Exploration

Private
Space Exploration

Kid's Library of Space Exploration

Kid's Library of Space Exploration

Private
Space Exploration

C.F. Earl

Kid's Library of Space Exploration: Private Space Exploration

Village Earth Press
Vestal, New York 13850
www.villageearthpress.com

First Printing
9 8 7 6 5 4 3 2 1

Series ISBN (paperback): 978-1-62524-444-4
ISBN (paperback): 978-1-62524-409-3
ebook ISBN: 978-1-62524-044-6
    Library of Congress Control Number: 2014931529

Author: Earl, C.F.

Contents

ONE

What Is Private Spaceflight?

With a burst of fire, a thin, white rocket blasted off for space. A giant cloud of smoke covered the launch pad. The rocket launched from Cape Canaveral in May of 2012. National Aeronautics and Space Administration (NASA) rockets had been leaving Earth from the base for years—but this rocket was different. It wasn't a NASA rocket.

As the white rocket left the ground, with a trail fire behind it, people watching the launch could see "SPACEX" in black letters on it. This rocket wasn't owned by the government. A business named SpaceX had built it.

For the first time in history, a company owned by ordinary people had launched a spacecraft that was flying supplies to the International

A SpaceX Falcon 9 rocket lifts off from Cape Canaveral Air Force Station in Florida, carrying a Dragon capsule filled with cargo for the SpaceX 2 mission.

PRIVATE SPACE EXPLORATION

Space Station (ISS). The SpaceX Falcon 9 was carrying food, clothing, and computer parts. The mission was a test for SpaceX. The company had to prove to NASA that it could safely fly *cargo* to the astronauts on the ISS. For SpaceX and the company's *founder*, Elon Musk, the launch was the end of a lot of work. But the launch was also a new start for private space exploration.

"Public" vs. "Private"

When people call Falcon 9's flight to the ISS a *private* spaceflight, they don't mean it's a secret or that it's something done behind closed doors. In this case, "private" just means "not the government." A private company is one that is owned by a few people. Other people can't buy a part of a private company unless the owners agree to the deal.

Governments around the world were once the only groups in charge of space exploration. In the early 1960s, the Soviet government sent the first people into space. Yuri Gagarin traveled around the Earth. He was the first person to orbit the planet in 1961. Eight years later, NASA astronauts Neil Armstrong and Buzz Aldrin put an American flag in the dust on the moon's face. No person had ever stepped on moon before them.

All these *missions* were *public* spaceflight, meaning "by the government" or "for the people." In fact, for many years, it was against the law in

International Space Station

The International Space Station (ISS) is the largest space station ever created. The ISS is run by 15 countries working together. Astronauts travel to the station to conduct experiments and gather information. Companies like SpaceX hope to change how supplies are delivered to astronauts aboard the ISS by making those trips for NASA and other nations.

Cargo is the goods and supplies carried on a spaceship—not people.

A **founder** is a person who starts a company or organization.

Missions are tasks, like having a man walk on the moon, that people want to see happen.

In the Space Station Processing Facility at NASA's Kennedy Space Center in Florida, engineers prepare experiments for loading aboard the SpaceX Dragon capsule for launch to the International Space Station.

many countries for anyone *but* the government to send rockets into space. No private companies were allowed to build their own rockets or travel into space.

In the last thirty years, the Russian and American governments have changed their laws to allow private companies to explore space. The United States government has also spent less on space exploration. NASA has had to shut down most of its missions to space. Instead, NASA began working with other countries to send people and supplies to space. They've also begun working with private spaceflight companies.

Today, private spaceflight is changing the way people think about exploring space. And new companies like SpaceX are making giant leaps in the business.

The Falcon 9 Rocket

The Falcon 9 rocket is built to carry the Dragon spacecraft into orbit. Once in orbit, the Dragon docks with the ISS and delivers its cargo. The Falcon 9 made its first successful flight to the ISS in 2012. Since then, SpaceX has sent the rocket on missions to get the Dragon to the ISS two more times. For more on the Falcon 9, including how tall the rocket is and how much it can carry, visit spacex. com/falcon9.

Business in Space

Why would anyone start a private spaceflight company? Like all businesses, companies working in spaceflight want to make money. The main reason people start private spaceflight companies is to make what is called a profit. People like Elon Musk spend money to explore space to make more money back.

That doesn't mean, however, that businessmen like Elon aren't interested in other things. For many people working in private spaceflight, exploring space is a lifelong dream. Many are also interested in finding new things and building new kinds of *technology*. Private space exploration is still exploration, even if the main goal

Technology is something that humans invent to make something easier or go somewhere new.

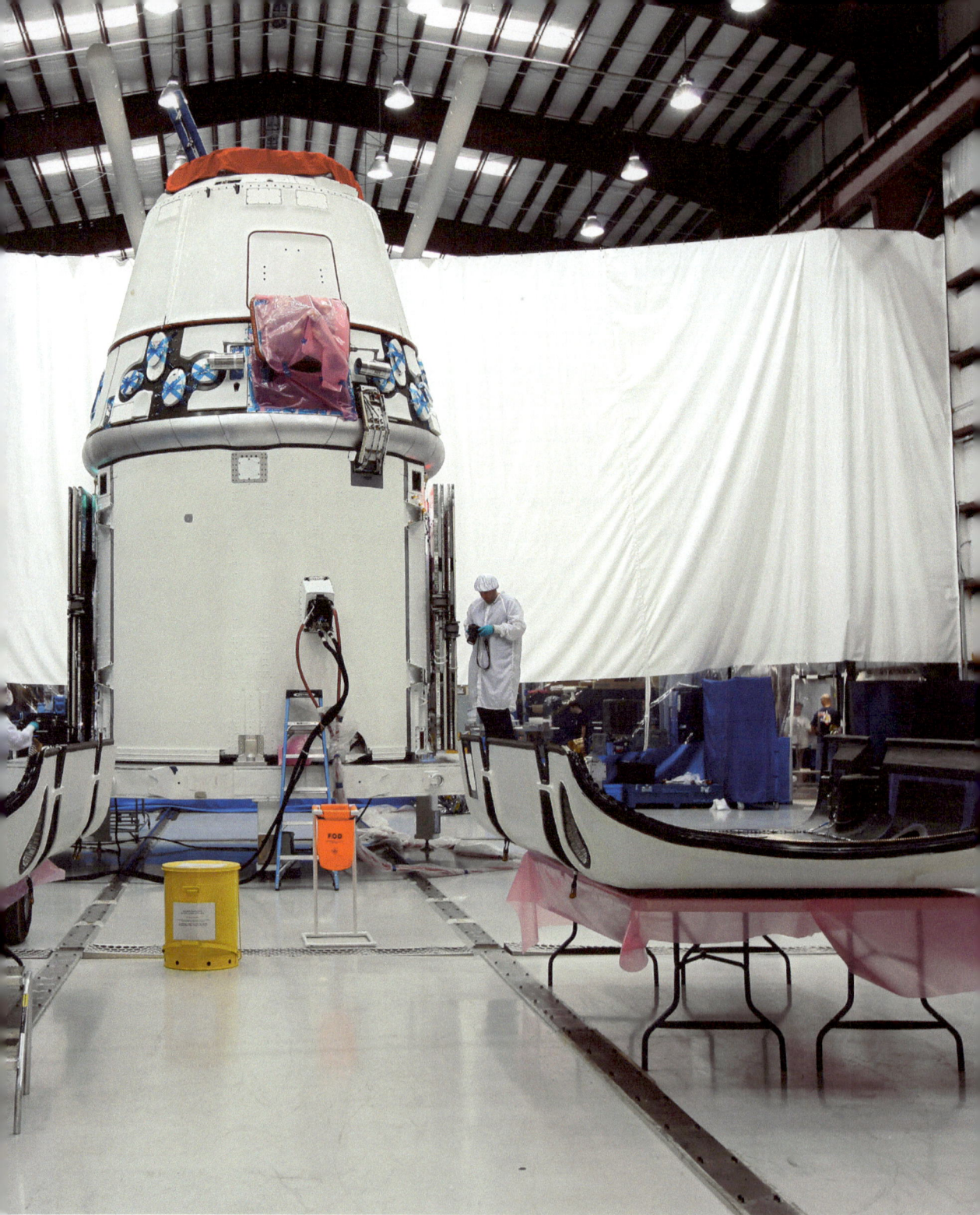

Workers prepare solar panels at the processing hangar used by Space Exploration Technologies, or SpaceX, at Cape Canaveral Air Force Station, Florida. The panels will provide power for the Dragon spacecraft that is being prepared for launch.

is making money. Like all explorers, it seeks to go to new places and find out new information. It's a quest for new discoveries.

Many space companies don't make much money today, but those companies are looking to the future. They are spending now to make a lot more money later. People are also still figuring out private spaceflight. Though many companies are coming into the business, it's still new. Things people think will make money now may not in the future. Other things no one has even thought of yet may make a few smart people a lot of money.

Today, private spaceflight companies are hoping to make money in a few different ways. Some companies, like SpaceX, want to work with governments. Now that NASA, for example, must look to other governments or companies like SpaceX to bring people into orbit, SpaceX hopes to make a lot of money working for NASA. SpaceX's owner hopes that government groups like NASA will turn to his company to take crewmembers to the ISS. Elon Musk is putting a lot of money on the idea that NASA will pay his company even more to fly people and cargo into space. Many other companies are working with the same idea. Bigelow Aerospace, for example, hopes to make building space stations and taking crews into space cheaper for government groups like NASA. When it comes to spaceflight, though, "cheaper" is still very costly! Bigelow Aerospace plans to charge between $25 million and $36 million for a stay on the company's future space station. Other companies are also planning to take tourists into space.

Public and Private

Here are a few examples of things that are public—and similar things that are private:

Public
- the United States Post Office
- parks in towns and cities
- roads and highways
- town buses and city subways

Private
- FedEx and UPS
- amusement parks like SixFlags, SeaWorld, or Disney World
- taxicabs

Orbit is circling around something else in space. Most satellites and space stations are in orbit around the Earth.

Since the Space Shuttles were retired in 2011, NASA started working with private companies to bring supplies up to the International Space Station. SpaceX's Dragon spacecraft, shown here, was the first private ship to successfully reach orbit and dock with the ISS.

Companies like Richard Branson's Virgin Galactic want to start taking passengers into **orbit** in just a few years. These companies hope people who have dreamed of going to space will pay big money for a ticket.

Plans aren't finished for taking people on space vacations just yet. But many companies are working on big ideas. The Golden Spike Company, for example, wants to sell tickets to the moon. The company has said it will take tourists, scientists, or anyone else who wants to make the journey. That's if you can afford the price. A vacation away from planet Earth is going to cost a lot of money!

A few companies aren't trying to get things *off* Earth into space. Instead, they want to bring what's in space *back* to Earth and sell it here. Planetary Resources, Inc. has plans to mine *asteroids* for metal or water and bring them back to planet Earth. It may sound crazy, but the company has big plans and millions of dollars to spend.

Many ideas in private spaceflight sound like something you'd read in stories. Just a few years ago, the idea of a private spaceflight company seemed silly. Today, companies like Elon Musk's SpaceX are helping to build a new future for space exploration.

Companies in Space Today

Many companies already have satellites in space. Radio companies XM and Sirius both have satellites in orbit. These companies are sending music and talk radio across the world using satellites. Cell phone companies work with businesses that send satellites into orbit to make sure customers can always call their friends and family.

Asteroids are large chunks of rock and metal floating through space—but not large enough to count as planets.

Find Out Even More

Reading books like this one is a great way to learn about subjects like space exploration. Books can hold a lot of amazing information. The authors have found facts they thought readers would want to know. Authors put facts and stories about their subjects together in a way that will make sense for readers. But books aren't perfect. No one book can hold all the information about a subject. To get a better view of a subject, you'll have to read more than one book.

Whether you want to read about rockets in space or anything else, you should start either at your school library or the nearest public library. At the library, you can find books by looking in the card catalog. Many libraries have a computer card catalog. If you have any trouble finding books, ask the librarian for help you find what you're looking for.

Try looking for some of the books listed here:

Floca, Brian. *Moonshot: Space Exploration*. New York: DK Eyewitness Books, 2009.

Thimmesh, Catherine. *Team Moon: How 400,000 People Landed Apollo 11 on the Moon*. New York: Houghton Mifflin, 2006.

If you can't find any books on this list at your library, you can probably find other books about space exploration. Take a look at the pages of the books you find in the library. In the front of the book, you'll probably see the table of contents. Find a chapter that stands out to you and flip to that page. Read over a few of the pages. Flip through other pages in the book and look at the index or glossary. After taking a look over some of the pages of the book, ask yourself these questions:

1. Do you understand the information in the book? Finding a book that you understand is a big part of reading well. Not every book is right for every reader. Make sure you understand what you're reading. But don't forget to challenge yourself a little bit! Find the right mix for you.
2. How is the book organized? Can you use the table of contents to find information easily? Does the book have an index to help? What about a glossary to better understand the words in the book?
3. Are there any facts in the book you haven't read in another book about space exploration?
4. Are there pictures in the book? How do they help you understand the subjects in the book?
5. Do you like the book? Why? What don't you like about the book? Would you read the rest of the book?

TWO

Early History

On the day of the historic Falcon 9 launch, NASA Administrator Charles Bolden couldn't have been more excited. He told news reporters that the launch was a "new future" for spaceflight. He said it was a very important day.

In 2011, just a year before the SpaceX flight, NASA had *retired* its own space shuttle program. NASA wouldn't launch any more missions to space on its own. From now on, NASA would have to work with other countries or with companies like SpaceX. The 2012 Falcon 9 launch was one of the first steps in that direction. And it was a big step!

Private spaceflight is a fast-moving business today. But it wasn't always that way. For many years, no private companies could launch rockets into space.

When something is **retired**, it is no longer used.

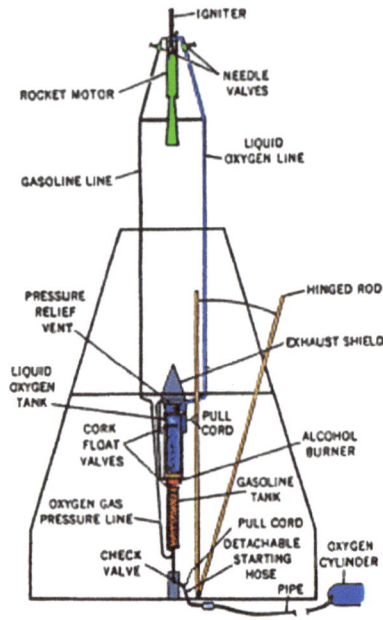

Dr. Robert Goddard's rocket designs may have seemed simple compared to the spacecraft we have today, but without his advances we could never have voyaged as far into space as we have.

Not too long before that, there weren't even rockets to launch. Over the last hundred years, a lot has changed in space exploration. And all of those changes have led to the success of new companies like SpaceX.

The Beginning of Private Space Exploration

The first private spaceflight began in the 1920s. In 1925, Daniel Guggenheim gave $250,000 to New York University. He told the university to start a school of *aeronautics*. In 1926, he spent more than $2 million to start a group to fund aeronautics *research*. That same year, a scientist named Robert Goddard launched a rocket he built himself. It shot more than 40 feet (a little more

Aeronautics is the science of how things travel through the air.

Research is study and experiments done to learn new science and invent new technologies.

than 12 meters) in the air. Goddard believed rockets could go much higher, however. He thought rockets might one day be used for travel into space. Pretty soon, the two men, Guggenheim and Goddard, started working together.

The Rise of Private Spaceflight

In the 1950s and '60s, the U.S. government and the Soviet Union (what today we call Russia) were locked in a race. Each country wanted to be the first into space and then the first to the moon. Both governments spent a lot of money to beat the other. Along the way, people on Earth learned a lot about space and a lot about the Earth. We saw the Earth from space for the first time ever. We saw human footprints on the moon. But during all this time, only governments explored space. No private groups, no regular people, could launch anything into space.

Then, in 1962, a new law allowed companies to send satellites into space. The government still helped these companies get their satellites into orbit, but the first companies had made it into space.

Over time, many governments, including the U.S. government, had less money to spend on space exploration. Problems on the Earth used up most of the governments' money. Many people

Early Private Space Explorers

People began giving money to space exploration as far back as the late nineteenth century. But early private space explorers didn't even get off the ground. Without rocket technology, space exploration meant using telescopes to look up at the night sky. The first private explorers often spent money on building observatories. Observatories are buildings made to hold powerful telescopes. People use these telescopes to study the sky and the weather. Before rockets, people used observatories to explore space from Earth.

In the late 1800s, a man from Chicago name Charles Tyson Yerkes made a lot of money. He had made his money building streetcars, but now he gave hundreds of thousands of dollars to the University of Chicago so the school could build an observatory. The Yerkes Observatory opened in 1897. About twenty years earlier, in California, James Lick had done something similar. He gave money to the University of California to build what was then the world's most powerful telescope.

Sputnik was the first object humans ever put into orbit around the Earth. Without it, companies today might not be putting their own ships into space!

PRIVATE SPACE EXPLORATION

When Ronald Reagan signed the Commercial Space Launch Act in 1984, it meant that any company was allowed to put a satellite into space, not just NASA. Many technologies today could not have existed without this law, including satellite television, GPS, and satellite Internet.

began to wonder whether governments were the best organizations to explore space. Maybe, people thought, businesses might be better at exploring space. Governments could save money they had been spending on costly missions to space. And companies could spend their own money to risk space travel.

Beginning in the 1980s, the private spaceflight business began to take shape. In Germany, the company OTRAG was one of the first to build its own rockets. In Europe, several countries came together to form Arianespace, a France-based spaceflight company. Then in 1984, the

Using special planes, you can get a few moments of zero gravity without needing to go to outer space. Here, an astronaut trains in his spacesuit for what it will be like to take a trip on the Space Shuttle.

Eventually, NASA started trusting private companies to build rockets and spacecraft for them. This is the Athena rocket, built by Lockheed Martin, which took a probe to the moon!

U.S. president Ronald Reagan signed a law that gave people outside the government the right to launch spacecraft.

In the 1990s, Russian spaceflight companies began taking over the country's space exploration. In the United States, NASA started buying more parts and equipment from private companies. Private companies like Boeing and Lockheed Martin worked hard to earn NASA's trust— and the U.S. government's money.

In the late 1990s and early 2000s, many private spaceflight companies began working on ideas for their own rockets, launches, and missions into space. Many of these companies began to see a chance

Barack Obama's suggestion that private companies take over sending ships to the International Space Station would help save NASA time and money—and let them focus on other exciting projects, like journeying to Mars!

to make money working with governments. Others saw a future where travelers could pay for trip off the planet. Businesspeople from around the world saw that money could be made in space exploration. Google even offered a 20-million-dollar reward—the Lunar XPRIZE—to any group that could put a spacecraft on the moon.

In 2010, President Barack Obama gave a speech saying the United States should stop sending astronauts into space. Instead, the President said, NASA should work with private companies to explore space. Companies like Elon Musk's SpaceX were ready to answer the President's challenge. The private spaceflight business had become a reality.

Find Out Even More

When you're searching for more information about your favorite subjects, the Internet is a great tool. While books can only hold so much information, there is no limit to the information you can find online.

Using a search engine like Google or Bing can help you narrow down your search. Search engines help to sort through all the information on the Internet. By searching for key words, you can find almost anything online using search engines. Key words are short groups of words that give search engines an idea of the kind of information you're looking for.

Try searching for some of the key words below using Google.com:

NASA
Charles Bolden
Buzz Aldrin
Neil Armstrong
Yuri Gagarin
private spaceflight
SpaceX
Falcon 9
Elon Musk

You'll never be able to read everything there is online about Elon. Google finds more than 69 million results for "Elon Musk"! But search engines bring the best results to you first, so you'll usually find the best websites about Elon Musk on the first few pages of your search results.

Search engines can only bring you results based on your search results. So this means that what you search for is important. Make sure to choose your key words carefully. Being specific is the best way to find exactly what you're looking for. The wrong key words can take you to websites with nothing about the subjects you want to read about. And always remember, spelling can be very important when searching for information online.

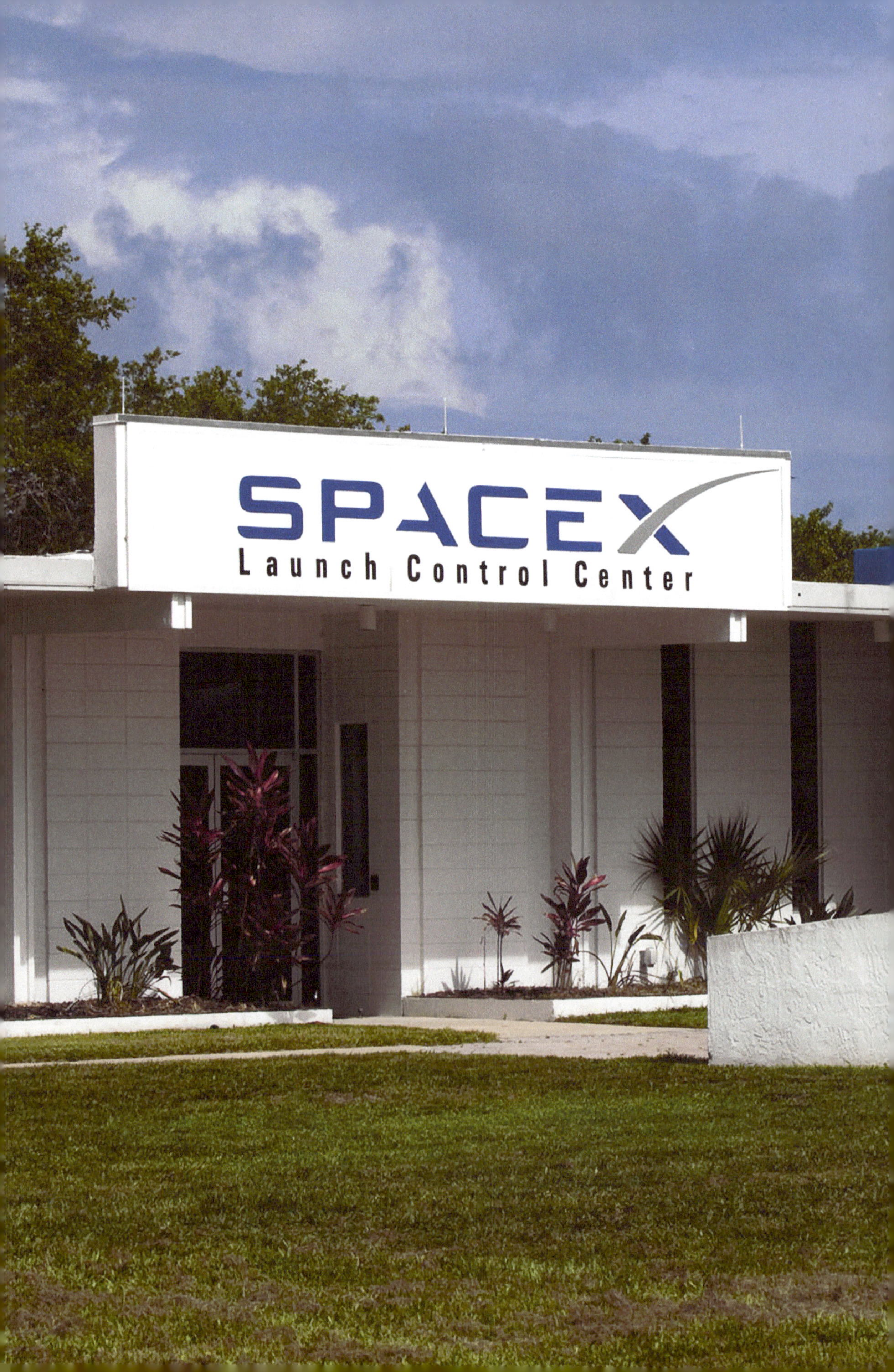
SPACEX
Launch Control Center

THREE

SpaceX and Virgin Galactic

SpaceX's big flight in 2012 was an end and a beginning. For many, it was the start of a new kind of space travel. The launch was the beginning of new time for private spaceflight. But for SpaceX founder Elon Musk, the launch was also the end of years of hard work.

"People were really giving it their all," Musk said. "For us, it was like winning the Super Bowl."

Musk's company had worked for years with NASA. Now, the historic launch had a historic base to match it. Cape Canaveral has seen American rockets lifting off since the 1960s.

At the moment of the launch, SpaceX entered the history books. "Every bit of adrenaline in my body released at that moment," Musk told NASA. His company had become a leader in a new space race. This space race isn't between big governments like the United States and Russia. This new kind of race to the stars is between private spaceflight companies like SpaceX and their *competition*, other companies like them.

Your **competition** is the other people and companies that are trying to do the same thing you are, only better.

Elon Musk shakes hands with Charles Bolden, NASA administrator.

SpaceX

SpaceX hopes to be the leader in private spaceflight missions. They want to sell tickets to government groups like NASA for millions of dollars. The test flights that the company has been working on (like the 2012 launch from Cape Canaveral) are like auditions for later NASA missions. NASA's been watching and making sure that SpaceX does everything just right. When you get something wrong in spaceflight, things can get dangerous quickly. So NASA wants to be sure it's worth it to pay SpaceX for a ride to the ISS or into orbit.

Right now, SpaceX is only carrying supplies into space, no people. The company is still working on getting spaceflight right. SpaceX doesn't want to risk human lives before it's sure people can travel on SpaceX spacecraft safely.

SpaceX has a few different projects in the works. The Falcon 9 rocket is SpaceX's latest launch vehicle. That means that it's a machine that lifts off the Earth and travels to space. Once there, the Falcon 9 rocket is built for only one thing. The rocket is made to deliver another spacecraft to orbit. This second craft is called Dragon.

Dragon is made to bring people and cargo to space stations and back again safely. In 2012, SpaceX launched Dragon on a mission to the International Space Station. The Falcon9

Who Is Elon Musk?

Elon Musk was born on June 28, 1971, in Pretoria, South Africa. He started using computers when he very young. He sold his first computer program when he was twelve. When Elon was a teenager, he moved to Canada for college. He ended up in California, going to Stanford University. But he didn't stay long at Stanford either. He soon left school to go into business.

Elon founded his first company, Zip2, in his early twenties. He started the company with his brother and eventually sold the company for more than $300 million. In 2001, Elon started PayPal, a way to pay for the things you buy online. eBay bought PayPal for $1.5 billion in 2002, the same year that Elon started SpaceX. Then Elon co-founded car company Tesla Motors. Tesla makes electric cars. Later, Elon founded a solar power company called SolarCity. Today, Elon works at Tesla Motors, SolarCity, and SpaceX. He's worth about $2.7 billion. In 2013, he introduced a new idea called Hyperloop, a very fast train that Elon wants to build between San Francisco and Los Angeles. The train would travel more than 350 miles in less than an hour.

The Dragon spacecraft represents the closest a private company has come to putting humans in space. Here, Elon Musk and Charles Bolden present a model of the DragonRider, the part of Dragon that will carry astronauts.

President Obama is eager to see how far space exploration can go now that private companies are getting involved. Here, he takes a tour of SpaceX's launch pad with Elon Musk.

rocket brought Dragon into space carrying cargo for the ISS. After delivering its cargo, Dragon left the ISS and headed back to Earth safely. Before this, only governments had ever launched a mission that brought cargo to the space station and then brought cargo back.

SpaceX hopes to also bring people to the ISS with Dragon. The company built the spacecraft to carry people. SpaceX is working with NASA to make sure Dragon is ready to take people to space soon.

SpaceX is also working on plans for a new spacecraft called the Falcon Heavy. SpaceX calls the Falcon Heavy the "most powerful rocket

Richard Branson started off in the music industry, but he he also started successful businesses in many other industries. Today, he is helping to push forward humanity's progress in exploring space!

in the world." The company says that the rocket will make more missions to the moon possible (or even missions to Mars). In the future, SpaceX will also use the Falcon Heavy to send tourists to space, working with a few different companies as well.

SpaceX has big plans and big goals. The company is only just over ten years old, but it has already done more than most private spaceflight companies. SpaceX is definitely a leader in private spaceflight.

Virgin Galactic

SpaceX may be one of the most famous private spaceflight companies, but it's not the only one. Virgin Galactic, owned by billionaire Sir Richard Branson, is also making a name in private spaceflight.

Branson made his fortune with his Virgin Group. Virgin Group owns an airline, a record company, and a cell phone service company. In all, Virgin has thousands of workers and makes billions of dollars. In 2004, Virgin grew even more.

That year, a pilot named Mike Melville flew SpaceShipOne, a spacecraft launched from a plane. A company called Scaled Composites had built SpaceShip-One. The company was hoping to win the Ansari X Prize. After Mike Melville helped Scaled Composites win the Ansari X Prize, Branson signed an agreement with the company to build SpaceShipTwo. The plane that would

Who Is Sir Richard Branson?

Richard Branson was born on July 18, 1950, in London, England. His father worked as a lawyer. He went to good schools, but he wasn't a very good student. When he left school, Richard got to work in the music business. He started a business selling music with a few friends and called the company Virgin. In 1972, Richard helped start Virgin Records, a recording company. Later, in 1984, Richard started Virgin Airlines. In 1999, he founded Virgin Mobile, a cell phone company. He's sold all three companies for hundreds of millions of dollars and started many more using the Virgin name. In 1999, he was knighted by the Queen of England.

Today, Sir Richard Branson is one of the richest men in the world. He's very successful in business but also works on things more important to him than money. In the late 1980s, Richard traveled across the Atlantic Ocean in a hot air balloon! Richard also works to fight climate change and teach people about how to treat our planet with respect. He's broken a few world records for sailing around the world.

Most of NASA's ships have gotten to space by launching rockets right from the ground, but Virgin Galactic's approach is to fly its spacecraft high into the sky first using planes like this.

launch it was called WhiteKnightTwo. Together, Scaled Composites and Branson would build both the spacecraft and the plane. Branson called the new company Virgin Galactic. He hopes that Virgin Galactic will be the first to make real the dream of ordinary people traveling to space. Branson calls his company "the first spaceline."

Virgin Galactic tested SpaceShipTwo and WhiteKnightTwo. Launched from WhiteKnightTwo, SpaceShipTwo doesn't actually go into space. Instead, once passengers are on board, they will feel a few minutes of the kind of weightlessness astronauts feel in the low gravity of a mission in space. The flight lasts a few hours before tourists land safely. It's not quite walking on the moon, but it's the closest to exploring space that many people will ever get.

The company started selling tickets in 2005. Some very famous people have already got their seats on SpaceShipTwo booked. Angelina Jolie, Stephen Hawking, and Tom Hanks are all rumored to have signed up. The first tickets sold for $200,000, and hundreds of people bought them. Cheaper tickets on sale right now go for $100,000.

With big plans and lots of money to carry them out, Virgin Galactic is ready to become one of the biggest companies in private spaceflight.

Other Private Spaceflight Companies

SpaceX and Virgin Galactic aren't the only private companies heading toward space. Today, many companies are working in private space exploration. Here are just a few:

Blue Origin
www.blueorigin.com

Space Adventures
www.spaceadventures.com

Bigelow Aerospace
www.bigelowaerospace.com

Golden Spike Company
www.goldenspikecompany.com

Mars One
www.mars-one.com

Find Out Even More

Look over the sites that come up first when you search online for more information about space exploration. Not every search result is a good source of information, though. Each site is different, and you'll have to decide which sites are best.

Try searching for "SpaceX" on Google. You'll find millions of results, but look at the first page of results. You'll likely see some of the sites below come up first.

SpaceX
www.spacex.com

SpaceX: Wikipedia, the free encyclopedia
en.wikipedia.org/wiki/SpaceX

SpaceX (SpaceX) on Twitter
twitter.com/SpaceX

NASA: SpaceX Launch
www.nasa.gov/spacex

spacexchannel: YouTube
www.youtube.com/user/spacexchannel

Which of these sites will be the best source of information? Some sites will have better information than others, so you'll have to pick and choose.

SpaceX.com is probably the best source of information on the company. Companies build websites to share information about their histories and goals. They might share information about people who work at the company or how the company started. Company websites are a great way to find information about almost any company in the world. Official sites will have information straight from the companies themselves. But remember, these sites probably don't want to say anything bad about themselves. They may only include information that makes them look good, while they leave out facts that might make them look not so good.

NASA.gov is another good source of information. NASA.gov may be more objective about SpaceX than the company itself. "Objective" means that someone isn't influenced by personal opinions and feelings.

Social websites like Twitter and YouTube aren't always the best source of information. That's because anyone can say anything on these sites. Just because you see something on a social website doesn't mean it's necessarily true. You can check out these sites to see that pages that are run by SpaceX itself. On Twitter, accounts can be "verified" for companies, singers, politicians, or other important groups. This means you can be sure that information on the SpaceX Twitter page comes from SpaceX. Check for the blue checkmark on a Twitter page to see if it's verified. Social media websites can be good sources of information, but they aren't the first place to search for new information on space exploration or other topics.

Wikipedia can be another great place to get started when you're doing research—but always be sure to check for the small numbers near facts included on this website. When you click on these numbers, they'll lead to other websites from which the information was taken. That means you can follow a fact to make sure it came from a source that can be trusted. And if you don't see these links, then odds are good the information in that article may not be accurate. Since users create Wikimedia articles, not everything on Wikipedia is good information. Checking these facts yourself is an important part of using the site.

FOUR

The Future of Private Spaceflight

What if instead of taking a trip to your grandmother's house for summer vacation, you caught a ride to the moon? What if instead of a car trip with Mom and Dad to the Grand Canyon, you could buy a ticket to orbit the Earth? How about summer in orbit? Would you like to relax with a zero-gravity drink bubble?

Many people believe you will be able to book a trip to space sooner than you might think. At the time of the Falcon 9 launch, Elon Musk told reporters, "It's almost like being at the dawn of the Apollo era, but I think we'll go much farther than Apollo and really driving the technology to the point where almost anyone can go to space if they want to."

This bootprint, left by the Apollo 11 astronauts on the moon, is a part of our world's history. One day, though, it might not be only astronauts who go to the moon. If people like Elon Musk and Richard Branson have their way, one day tourists and colonists will be able to travel to the moon—and even other planets!

Richard Branson is ready for a future with vacations in space, too. And he wants to be the one to take you there. "I know there are literally thousands of people who would love to go to space, to be able to look out the window, to marvel at the beautiful Earth," Branson has said. "Through Virgin Galactic we will make it possible."

Vacations in space may be closer than you think.

Space Tourism

Virgin Galactic is one of the leaders in what's being called space *tourism*. The company wants to offer a taste of weightlessness to tourists who want to feel the thrill of space travel. Virgin wants to send the first ticket holders up on SpaceShipTwo in 2014.

Other companies have even bigger plans for space tourism. The Golden Spike Company, for example, wants to take tourists on trips to the moon. Golden Spike plans to use the Falcon Heavy rocket being built by SpaceX to sell trips to the lunar surface. Golden Spike says it hopes to land the first people to the moon by the year 2020. The company only wants to land two people at first, but Golden Spike has big ideas.

Space Adventures is another company working in space tourism. Space Adventures plans to offer many different kinds of trips. It has already had some of its customers spend time on the International Space Station. The

Moon Base?

Bigelow Aerospace wants to make money in some of the same ways that SpaceX does. The company plans to sell space tickets to NASA and other governments (or companies). But company founder Robert Bigelow has even bigger plans than that. He says he wants to build a base on the moon. Robert has also said he wants to make space stations to refuel spaceships traveling between Earth and the moon. Right now, Bigelow Aerospace has an agreement with NASA to work on new ideas for space exploration missions. Who knows? Maybe one day you'll be visiting your kids on the moon!

Tourism is when you travel to see a place where you don't live.

DR. RICHARD BRANSON

BRANSON GOES

GALACTIC

LIFTS OFF

VIRGIN'S SPACE-TRAVEL ADVENTURE

Why would a private company want to go to space? Lots of people wonder that, because it's so hard to make money doing it. For Richard Branson, the answer is tourism—he wants to make it affordable for regular people to get to the stars. Other companies are excited about the untapped resources in space—by mining asteroids and other planets, we could gather many resources that are much more scarce here on Earth.

company offers many different kinds of trips. Space Adventures even offers a ticket to the moon, though the company hasn't made the trip yet.

Private spaceflight companies give people who aren't astronauts the opportunity to travel from planet Earth. Companies like Virgin Galactic and others are giving people who've dreamed of traveling to space the chance to live those dreams. The future of space tourism has never been more exciting.

The Space Rush

Family trips to space aren't the only reason big companies are trying to get their rockets off the ground. For many companies, space exploration is about finding new things to bring back and sell on Earth. Today, these companies are racing to be the first to succeed in space.

In the past, people traveled hundreds of miles because they heard about rumors of people finding gold in the old West. Some made fortunes mining for gold on land that is part of California today. Today, many people see space travel as a new kind of gold rush.

One company has big plans for mining in space. The company is called Planetary Resources, and it wants to mine metal from asteroids. Its plans may sound like science fiction, but Planetary Resources is serious about making money from asteroid mining. Its owners say that there are thousands of asteroids that aren't too far from Earth. They want to find which of these asteroids is valuable and then send missions to mine the asteroids. The company's plans call for mining platinum and other precious metals from asteroids. The company also wants to mine water from asteroids. The company has a lot of money to make its plan work, too. The CEO of Google, Larry Page, and other famous businesspeople have invested their money in Planetary Resources. Sir Richard Branson of Virgin Galactic is an investor too. Planetary Resources doesn't plan to actually mine asteroids for many years, though. It has to overcome a few more challenges before it can begin bringing platinum back from space.

First, Planetary Resources will have to find asteroids that would be good for mining. The company needs to put telescopes into space to have the best view of asteroids that might hold valuable metals. The

One of Bigelow Aerospace's ideas is to create inflatable structures on other planets. These would be much cheaper to make and transport than solid metal structures. Here, Robert Bigelow demonstrates one of the prototypes to NASA's Lori Garver.

company will also need to work on better telescopes to make sure they're finding asteroids worth mining.

Planetary Resources has another problem as well. No country on Earth has laws about asteroid mining yet, because the question of who can mine which asteroids has never come up before. Until governments around the world decide how Planetary Resources is allowed to mine asteroids (and *if* the company can mine asteroids), the company will have to keep its ideas in the planning stages. If governments decide Planetary Resources' plan is legal, then the company can begin working to make it happen.

What's Next for Private Spaceflight?

Companies like Virgin Galactic and SpaceX are moving quickly to become leaders in the new space industry. Many companies have big ideas about making money in space. Some want to have tourists pay for a trip into orbit.

A Mars Reality Show?

Mars One plans to make money in a very different way from some of the other private spaceflight companies in business today. The company wants to send astronauts to Mars by the year 2023. Getting to Mars is very expensive, though, so the company will need a lot of money to make the mission work. So how will they make their money on a mission to the red planet? Mars One wants to make a reality television show about the journey. The show would star the astronauts on the mission. The company says the TV show would pay for the cost of the mission. Not everyone thinks the business will work. But if it does, you could be watching Mars One's reality show in the 2020s!

Others want to make money by bringing what's in space back to Earth. New companies are thinking of new ways to make money in space all the time. Many of these ideas seem a little strange at first, and some even sound silly. But new technology is making new ideas possible.

"I don't expect them all to succeed," says Michael Listner about these new ideas, "but I don't expect them all to fail." Michael is a lawyer who founded a company called Space Law & Policy Solutions. "Ten years ago, if you presented one of these plans, people would have looked

The groundbreaking of SpaceX's California launch site in 2011 was an exciting time for everyone interested in space exploration. The hard work of private companies like SpaceX will help humans go even further into the stars.

at you like you're crazy," Michael told *Wired Magazine*. "Now people can say, well it's a little crazy, but [after] what's been done, it might be possible."

No one can be sure what the future holds for space exploration—but private companies will be at the center of many of the most important breakthroughs. The years ahead are bound to be exciting!

Find Out Even More

Every site online is different. You have to judge each site you visit to decide whether the site is a good source of information.

Sites like Facebook and Twitter can be a great way to stay in touch with friends—but they aren't usually good sites for research about space exploration. Personal blogs are another kind of site that might not always be the best source of information. Each site is made for a different reason.

When searching for information online, ask yourself these questions about the sites you visit to decide whether they are good sources of information:

1. Who made the site? You can usually find out who made the site by checking the very top of the front page or the very bottom. On spacex.com, it's easy to tell that SpaceX runs the website, for example. Not every site is so easy, so you may have to dig a little to find who made the site you're visiting.
2. Is the site you're reading an official site? Is it a site made by a company or other kind of group? Did a person make it?
3. Why did the person or company make the site? Is the individual or company trying to sell something, for example? Or is the primary goal simply to teach people about a certain topic? Is the person or company trying to persuade people to think or believe a certain way?

4. Is the information you're reading up-to-date? Can you find newer information on other sites? Look for a date on every article or site you check out online. Usually, you want the most recent information, especially when you're looking for information about subjects in science or space exploration. If the site you're reading isn't up-to-date, you can always find another site.

5. Is the site easy to use? Can you find new information on the site easily? How is the site organized? Does the site have a search bar to help you find just what you're looking for? Some sites may be good sources of information but still be difficult to use.

Here's What We Recommend

If you want to learn more about private space exploration, here are some good books and websites to get you started!

Online

NASA
www.nasa.gov

Planetary Resources
www.planetaryresources.com

Space Adventures
www.spaceadventures.com

Space.com: Private Spaceflight News
www.space.com/spaceflight/private-spaceflight

SpaceX
www.spacex.com

Virgin Galactic
www.virgingalactic.com

In Books

Ferguson Publishing. *Space Exploration (Discovering Careers for Your Future)*. New York: Ferguson Publishing, 2008.

Greve, Tom. *Thanks NASA! (Let's Explore Science)*. Vero Beach, Fla.: Rourke Publishing Group, 2012.

Jedicke, Peter. *Great Moments in Space Exploration (Scientific American)*. New York: Chelsea House, 2007.

Redmond, Shirley Raye. *Richard Branson: Virgin Mega-brand Mogul (Innovators)*. Farmington Hills, Mich.: Kidhaven, 2011.

Scott, Carole and DK Publishing. *Space Exploration*. New York: DK Eyewitness Books, 2009.

Index

About the Author

C.F. Earl is a writer living and working in Binghamton, New York. Earl writes on a range of topics, including pop culture, history, and health.

Picture Credits

36: Carrienelson1 | Dreamstime.com
38: Keith Bell | Dreamstime.com
42: Steve Mann | Dreamstime.com
46: *Wired* Magazine

All other images are from NASA or in the public domain. If any image has been inadvertently uncredited, please notify Village Earth Press, Vestal, New York 13850, so that rectification can be made for future printings.

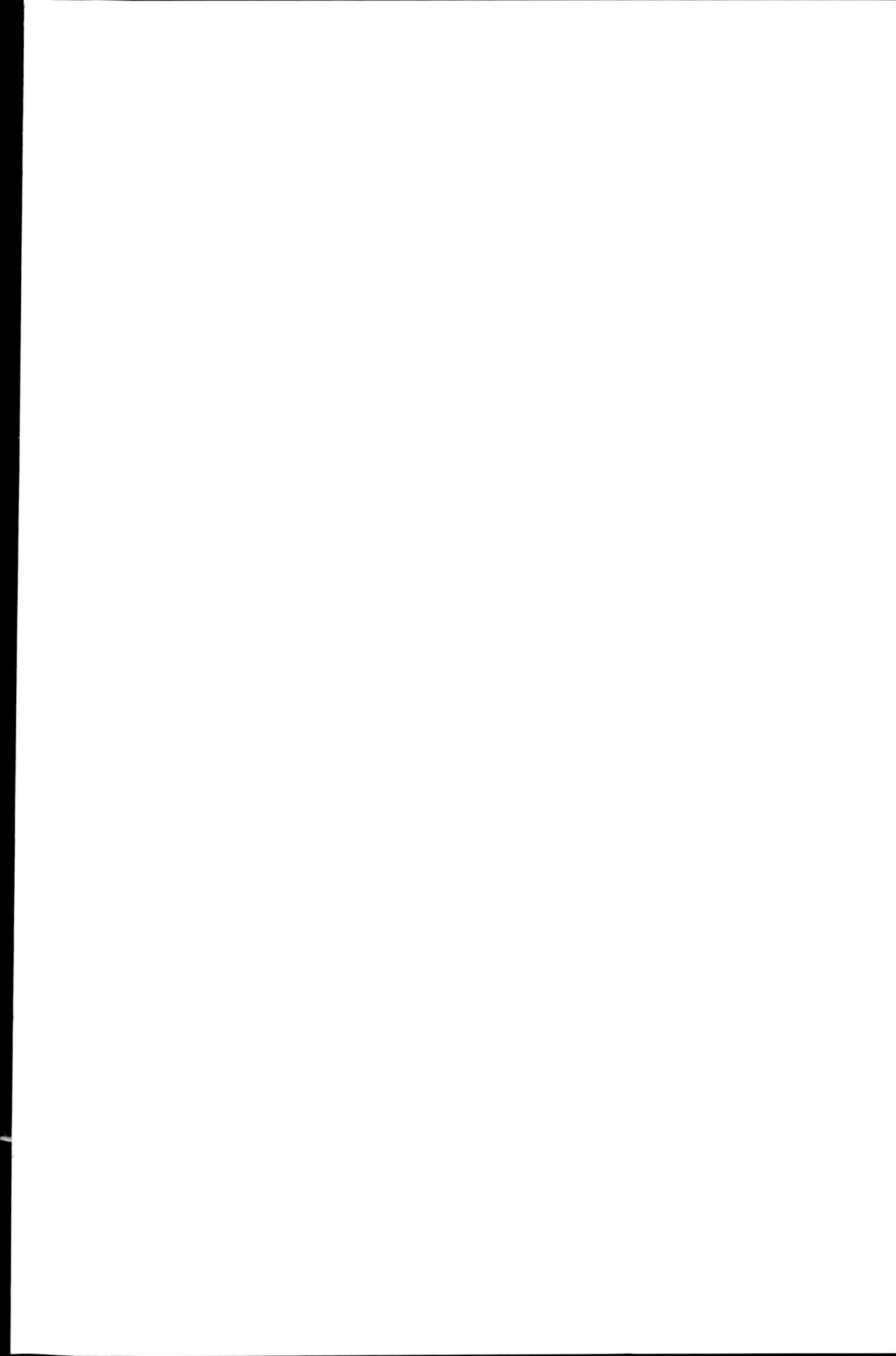

www.ingramcontent.com/pod-product-compliance
Lightning Source LLC
Chambersburg PA
CBHW042010080426

42734CB00002B/39